Yusuf/Cat Stevens

FOR UKULELE

Cover photo: A&M Records/Photofest

ISBN 978-1-4950-1081-1

HAL•LEONARD®
CORPORATION
7777 W. BLUEMOUND RD. P.O. BOX 13819 MILWAUKEE, WI 53213

Visit Hal Leonard Online at
www.halleonard.com

CONTENTS

Another Saturday Night

Words and Music by Sam Cooke

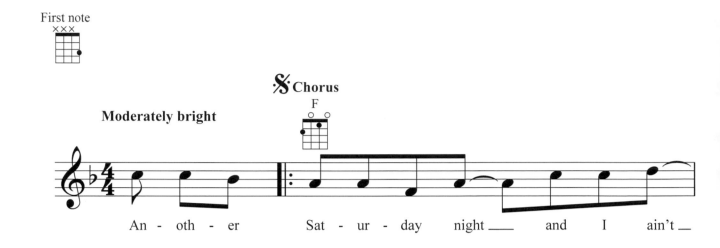

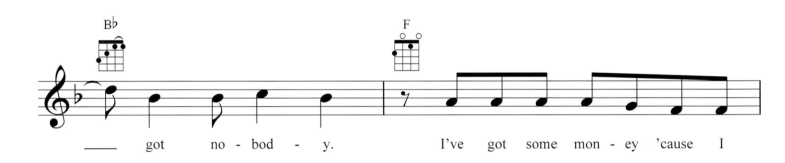

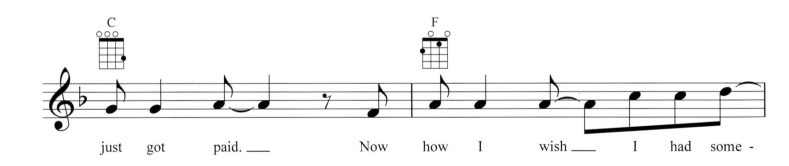

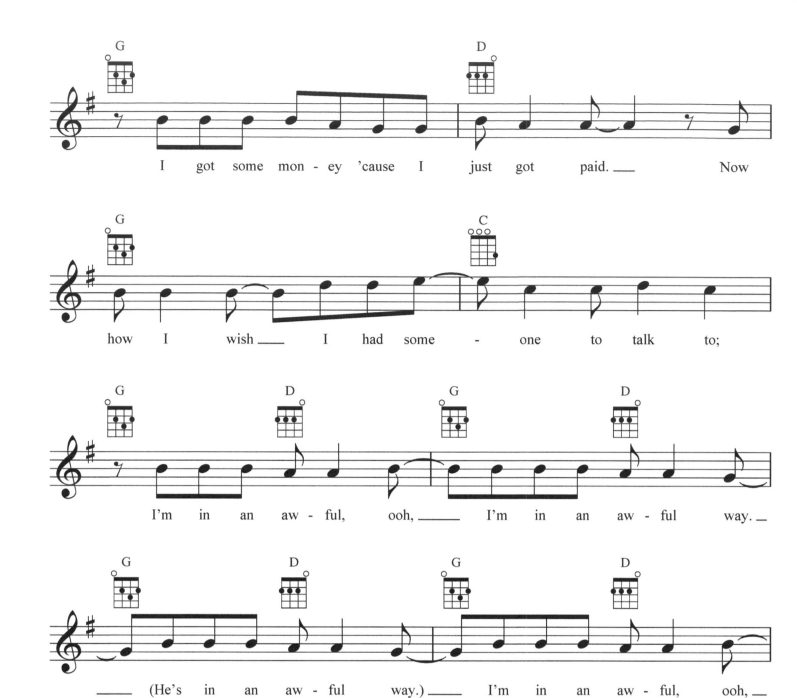

Additional Lyrics

2. Another fella told me he had a sister who looked just fine.
   Instead of being my deliverance, she had a strange resemblance
   To a cat named Frankenstein. Ooh, la, another... *(To Chorus)*

3. It's hard on a fella when he don't know his way around.
   If I don't find me a honey to help me spend my money,
   I'm gonna have to blow this town. Oh no, another... *(To Chorus)*

Father and Son

Words and Music by Cat Stevens

when you've found __ some - thing go - ing on. But take your time, __

__ think a lot. Why, think of ev - 'ry - thing __ you've got, __ for you __ will

still be here __ to - mor - row, but your dreams may not. 2. How can I __

Verse

__ try to ex - plain? __ When I do, __ he turns __ a - way __ a - gain. __ It's
(4.) __ that I cried, __ keep - ing all __ the things __ I knew __ in - side; __ it's

al - ways been the same, same old sto - ry. From the mo -
hard, __ but it's hard - er to ig - nore it. If they were right, __

- ment I __ could talk, I was or - dered __ to lis - ten. __ } Now there's a way, __
__ I'd __ a - gree, but it's them, __ they __ know, not me. __ }

Can't Keep It In

Words and Music by Cat Stevens

First note

Oh, I can't keep it in. I can't keep it in; I've

got - ta let it out. I've got - ta show the world; world's __

__ got - ta see, see all the love, love __ that's in me. I said,

why walk a - lone? Why wor - ry when it's warm o - ver here?

You've got so much to say; say __ what you mean, mean __

I'm up _____ for your love; love _____ heats my blood, blood _

Interlude

_____ spins my head and my head _____ falls in love, _ oh.

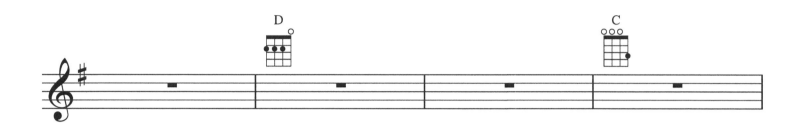

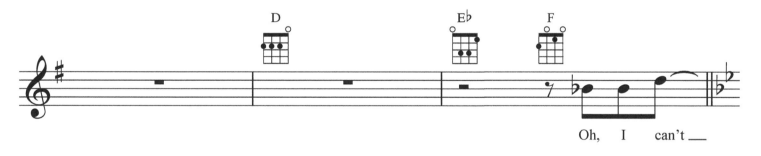

Oh, I can't _

Chorus

_____ keep it in. I can't keep it in; I've got-ta let it out.

I've got - ta show the world; world's _____ got-ta know,

know of the love, love ____ that lies low. So, why can't you say?

If you know, then why can't you say? You've got

too much de-ceit; de-ceit ____ kills the light. Light ____ has to shine; I said shine __

Verse

____ light, shine __ light. 2. Love, _____ that's no way to

live your life. _____ You al-low too much to go by, _____

_____ and that won't do. _____ No. _____

13

Lov - er,   I   wan - na have you   here   by ___ my side.

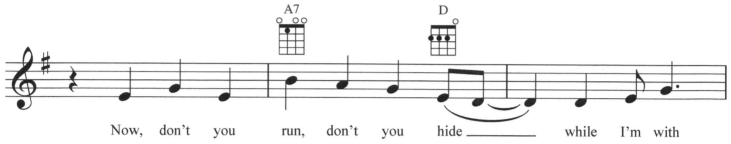

Now,   don't   you   run,   don't   you   hide _____   while   I'm   with

D.S. al Coda

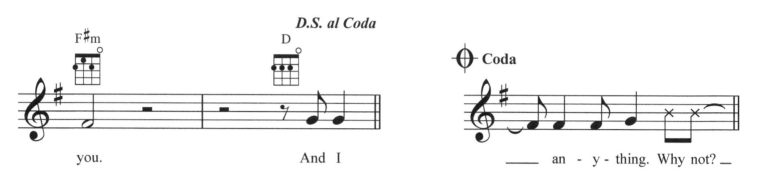

you.   And I   ___ an - y - thing. Why not? __

Outro

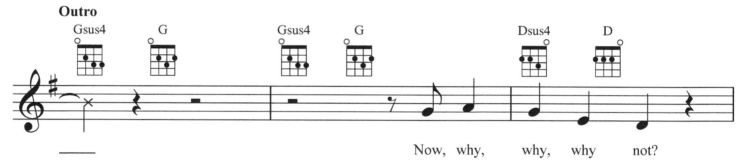

___   Now, why,   why,   why   not?

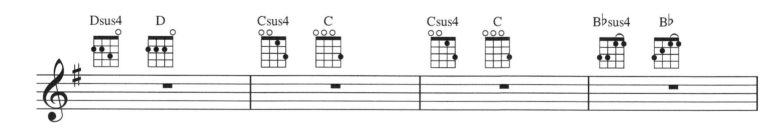

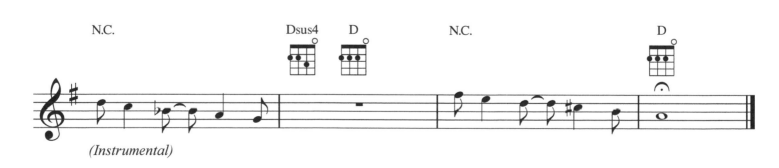

(Instrumental)

The First Cut Is the Deepest

Words and Music by Cat Stevens

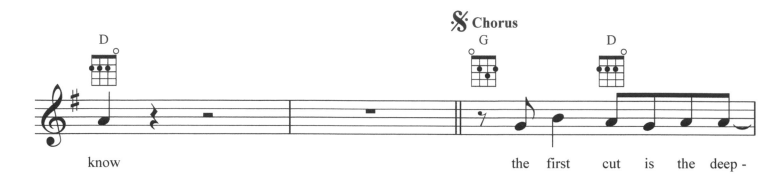

know

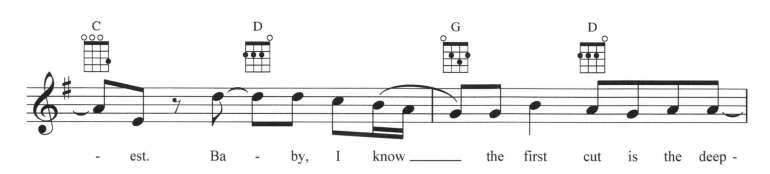

- est. Ba - by, I know _____ the first cut is the deep -

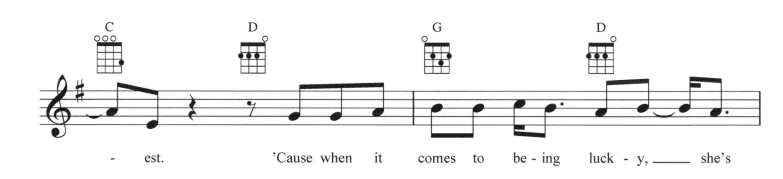

- est. 'Cause when it comes to be - ing luck - y, _____ she's

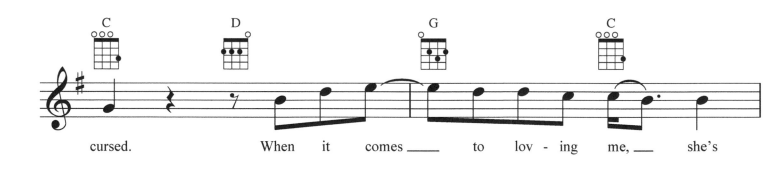

cursed. When it comes _____ to lov - ing me, __ she's

worst. _____ But when it comes to be - ing loved, she's _____

At the top right: %. Chorus

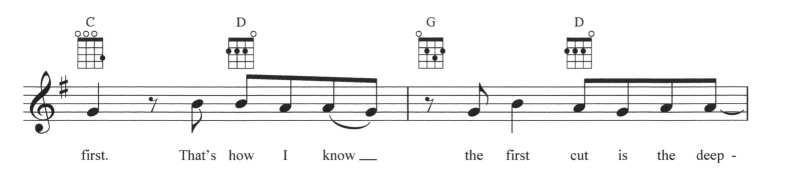

first. That's how I know ___ the first cut is the deep -

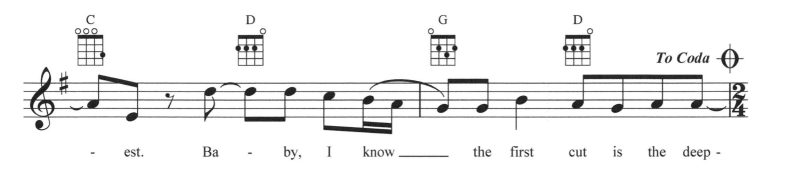

- est. Ba - by, I know _____ the first cut is the deep -

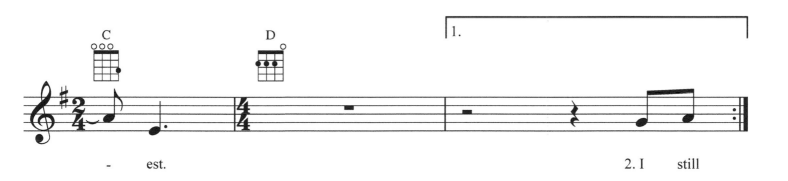

- est. 2. I still

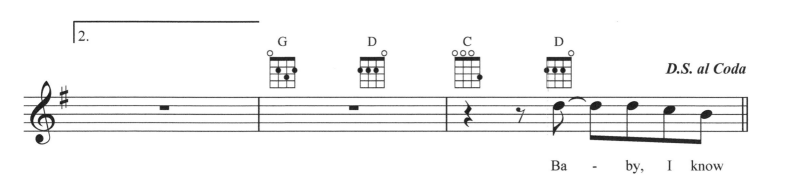

Ba - by, I know

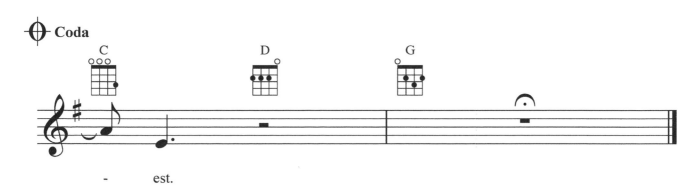

- est.

I Was Raised in Babylon

Words and Music by Yusuf Islam

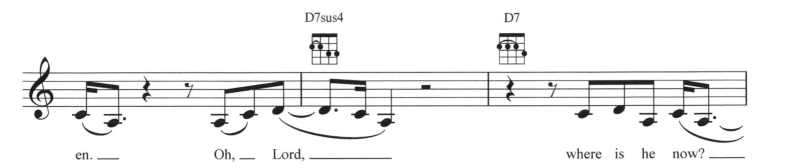

en. ___   Oh, ___ Lord, _____   where is he now? ___

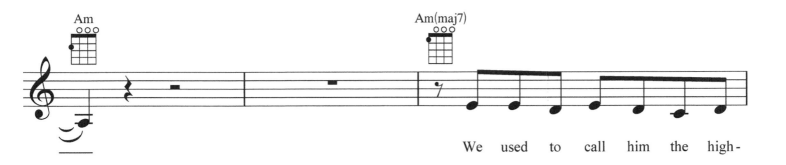

_____   We used to call him the high -

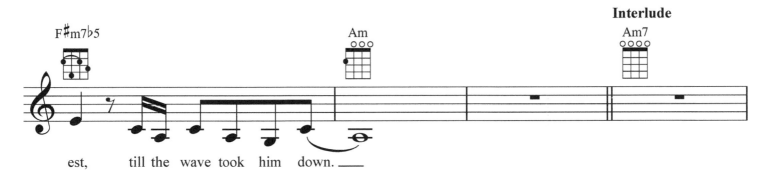

est,   till the wave took him down. ___

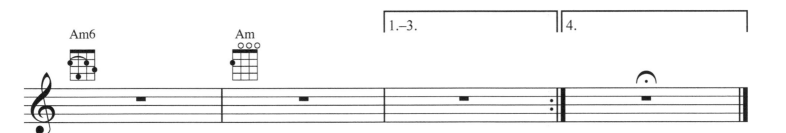

Additional Lyrics

3. I was born in the Holy Land;
   They told me it was by God's command.
   Oh, where are the others from?
   I thought that we were the chosen;
   I must have been wrong.

4. I loved to march with the Sultan
   And his diamond turban.
   Oh, Lord, then the world took hold.
   Let go the rope of God
   For a handful of gold.

5. I used to serve the empire
   On which the sun set never.
   Oh, now times have turned.
   We thought our white skins would save us;
   Then we got burned.

If You Want to Sing Out, Sing Out

Words and Music by Cat Stevens

Outro

want to sing out, ___ sing out. ___   And if you want to be free, be free.

___ ___   'Cause there's a mil - lion things ___ to be. ___

___ ___   You know that there are, ____ you know that there are, ___

___ you know that there are, ___ you know that there are, ____

___ you know that there are. ____

Hard Headed Woman

Words and Music by Cat Stevens

one who'll make ___ me do ___ my best. _____

And if I find ___ my hard ___ head-ed wom-an, ___

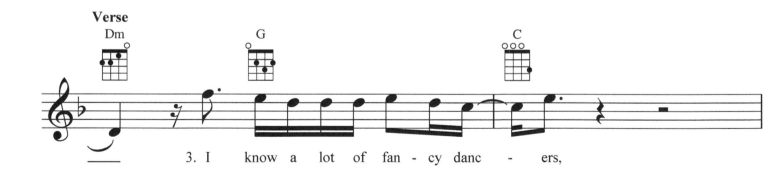

I know the rest of my life ___ will be blessed, yes, yes, yes. _____

Verse

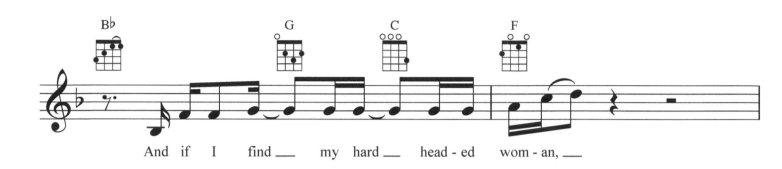

___ 3. I know a lot of fan-cy danc - ers,

peo-ple who can glide you ___ on a floor. _____

They move so smooth, _ but have no an - swers, _ whoa, _____

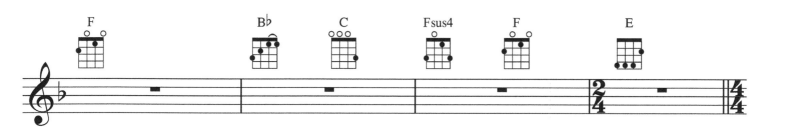

Interlude

_____ when you ask, "Why'd you come here for? Why?"

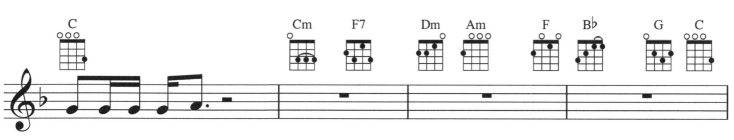

(Hard head - ed wom - an.)

Bridge

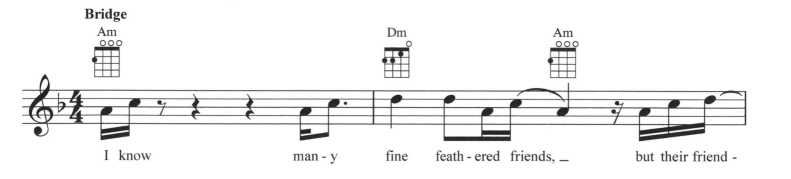

I know man - y fine feath - ered friends, _ but their friend -

- li - ness de - pends _ on how __ you do. They know man - y

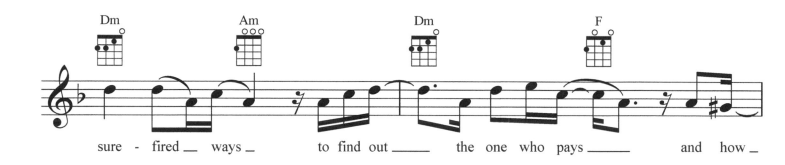

sure - fired _ ways _ to find out ___ the one who pays ____ and how _

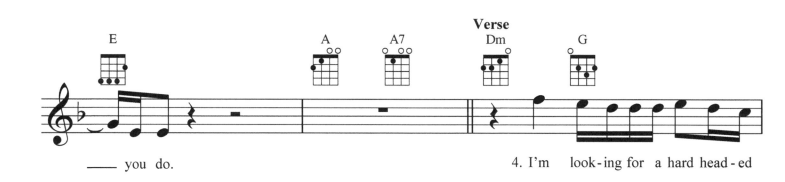

Verse

__ you do. 4. I'm look-ing for a hard head-ed

wom-an, one who will make _ me _ feel so good. _____

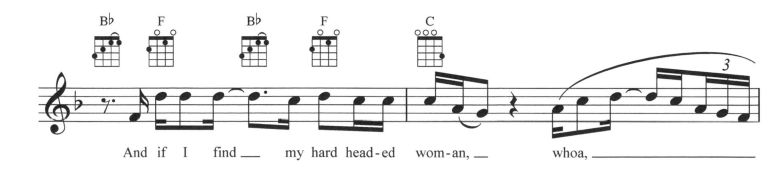

And if I find __ my hard head-ed wom-an, _ whoa, _____

I know my life will be as ___ it should, yes, yes, yes. _____

Outro-Verse

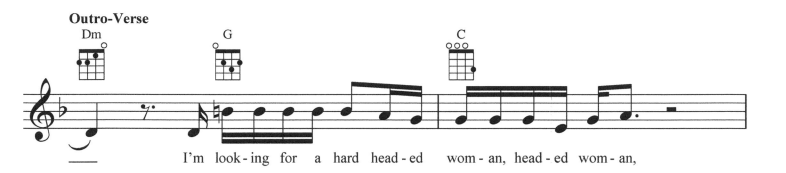

___ I'm look-ing for a hard head-ed wom-an, head-ed wom-an,

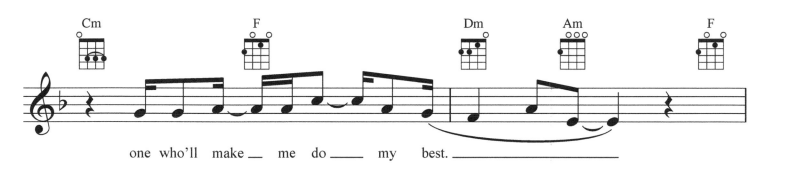

one who'll make ___ me do ___ my best. _____

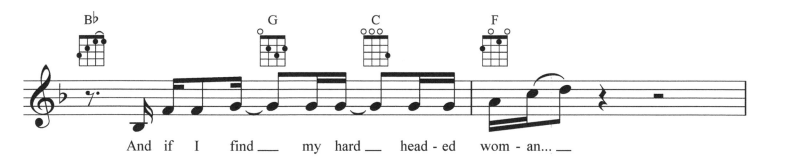

And if I find ___ my hard ___ head-ed wom-an... ___

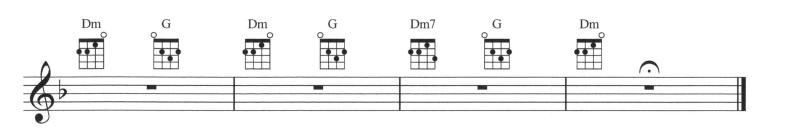

Maybe There's a World

Words and Music by Yusuf Islam

First note

Verse
Moderate Ballad

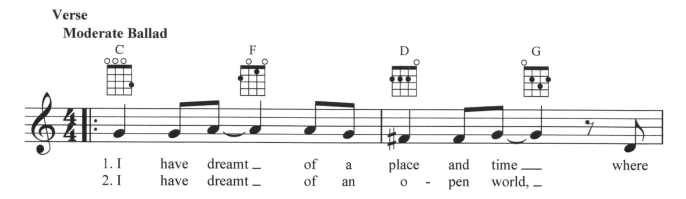

1. I have dreamt ___ of a place and time ___ where
2. I have dreamt ___ of an o - pen world, ___

no - bod - y gets ___ an - noyed.
bor - der - less ___ and wide,

But I
where the

must ad - mit ___ I'm not there yet, ___ but
peo - ple move ___ from place to place, ___ and

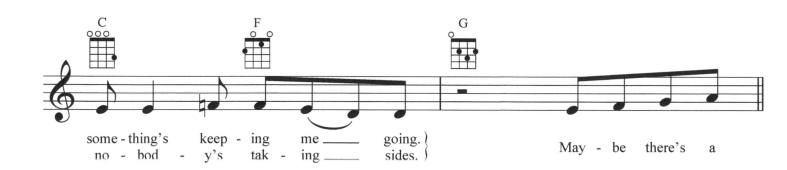

some - thing's keep - ing me ___ going. }
no - bod - y's tak - ing ___ sides. }

May - be there's a

How _____ nice! _____
How _____ nice! _____

Interlude

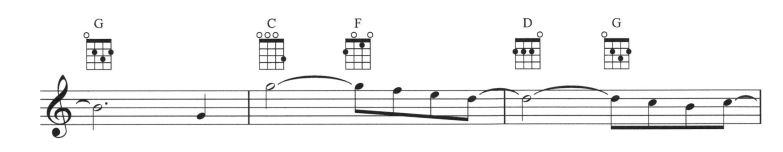

(Instrumental)

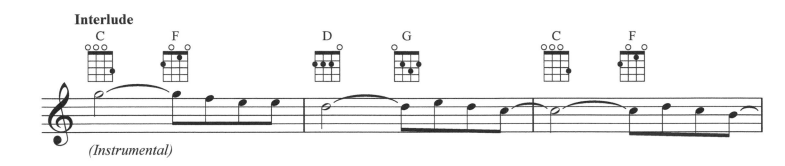

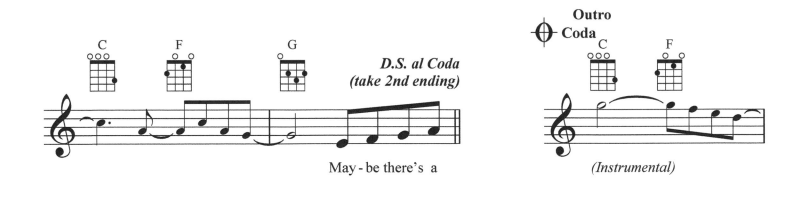

D.S. al Coda
(take 2nd ending)

May - be there's a

Outro
Coda

(Instrumental)

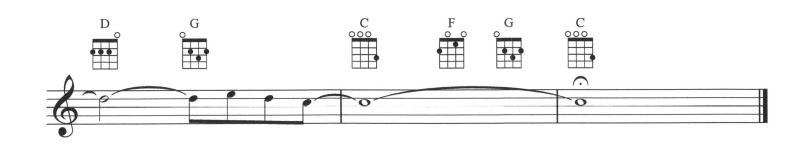

Miles from Nowhere

Words and Music by Cat Stevens

First note

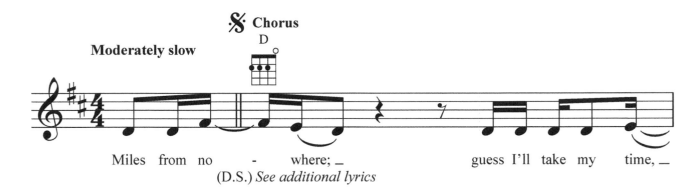

Moderately slow

S: **Chorus**

Miles from no - where; _

(D.S.) *See additional lyrics*

guess I'll take my time, _

_____

oh yeah, _

to reach there. _

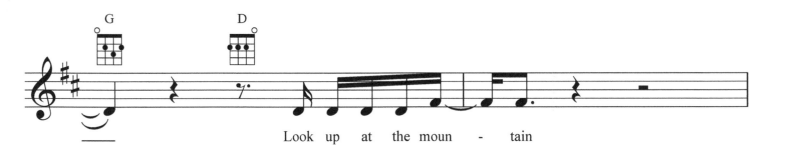

_____

Look up at the moun - tain

I have to climb, _____

oh yeah, _

to reach there. _____

Lord, my bod - y _____ has been a good

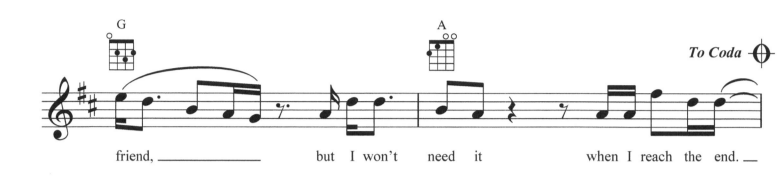

To Coda ⊕

friend, _____ but I won't need it when I reach the end. __

_____ Miles from no - where; I guess I'll take __ my

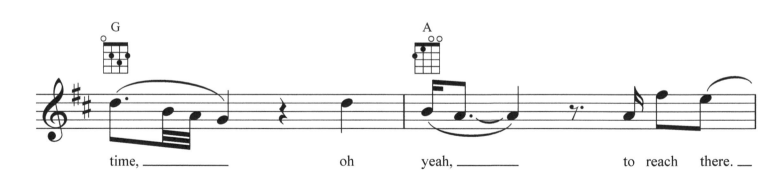

time, _____ oh yeah, _____ to reach there. __

Faster

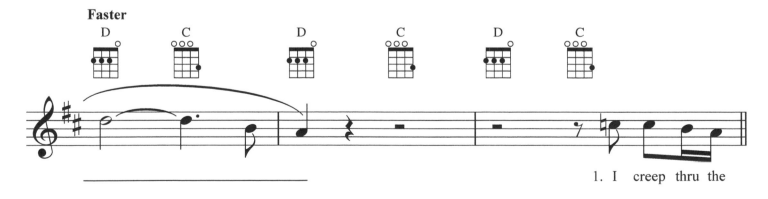

_____ 1. I creep thru the

Verse

val - leys　　and I grope thru the　　woods, __　　'cause I know when I

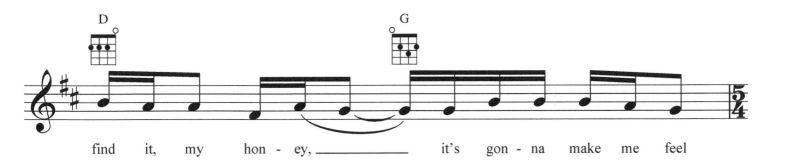

find it, my hon - ey, _____ it's gon - na make me feel

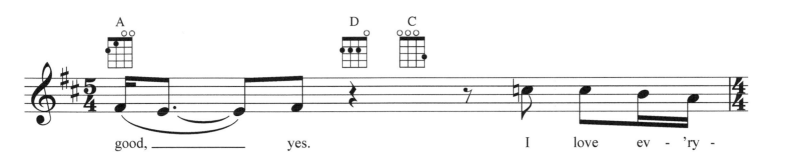

good, _____ yes.　　I　love　ev - 'ry -

thing, __　　so don't it make you feel　sad? __　　'Cause I'll drink to you, __

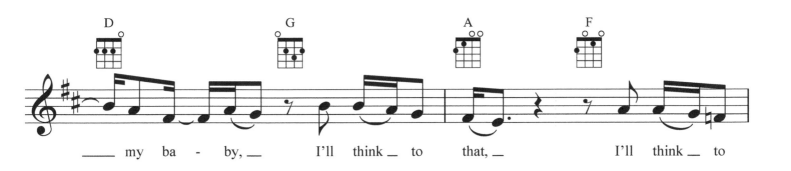

__ my ba - by, __　　I'll think __ to that, __　　I'll think __ to

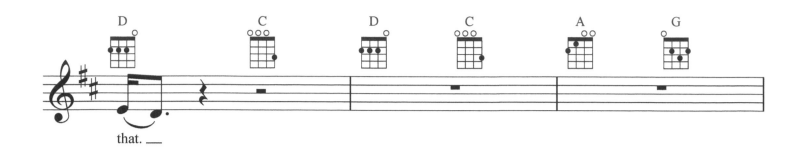

that. ___

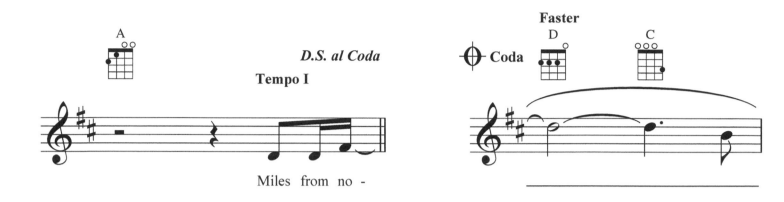

D.S. al Coda

Tempo I

Faster

⊕ **Coda**

Miles from no -

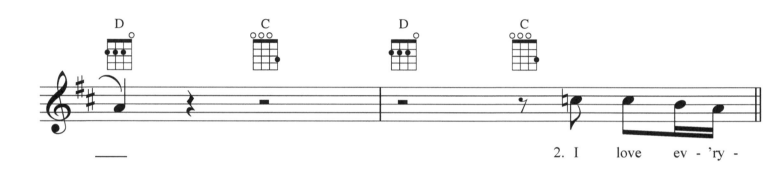

___

2. I love ev - 'ry -

Verse

thing, ___ so don't it make you feel sad? ___ 'Cause I'll drink to you, ___

___ my ba - by, ___ I'll think ___ to that, ___ I'll think ___ to

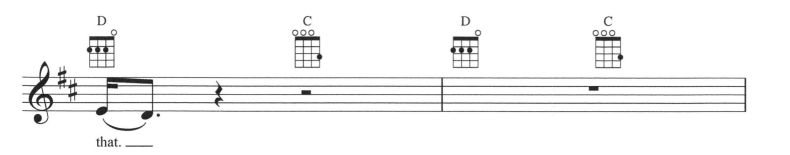

that. ____

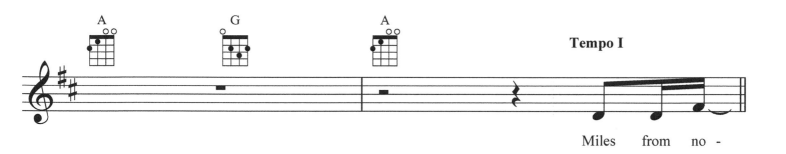

Tempo I

Miles   from   no -

Outro-Chorus

- where; __   guess I'll take my time, _____   oh

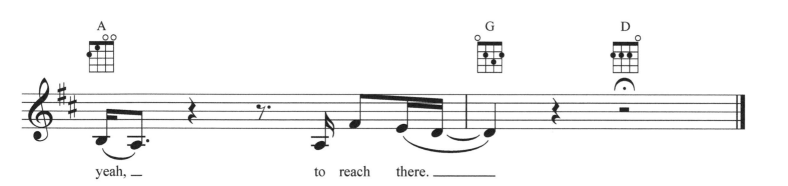

yeah, __   to reach   there. _____

Additional Lyrics

Miles from nowhere; not a soul in sight,
Oh yeah, but it's all right.
I have my freedom; I can make my own rules,
Oh yeah, the ones that I choose.
Lord, my body has been a good friend,
But I won't need it when I reach the end. *(To Coda)*

Moon Shadow

Words and Music by Cat Stevens

Outro-Chorus

I'm be-ing fol-lowed by a moon shad-ow, moon shad-ow, moon shad-ow.

Leap-in' and hop-pin' on a moon shad-ow, moon shad-ow, moon shad-ow,

moon shad-ow, moon shad-ow, moon shad-ow, moon shad-ow.

Additional Lyrics

2. And if I ever lose my eyes,
   If my colors all run dry;
   Yes, if I ever lose my eyes,
   Oh, if...
   I won't have to cry no more.

3. And if I ever lose my legs,
   I won't moan and I won't beg.
   Oh, if I ever lose my legs,
   Oh, if...
   I won't have to walk no more.

4. And if I ever lose my mouth,
   All my teeth, north and south;
   Yes, if I ever lose my mouth,
   Oh, if...
   I won't have to talk.

One Day at a Time

Words and Music by Yusuf Islam

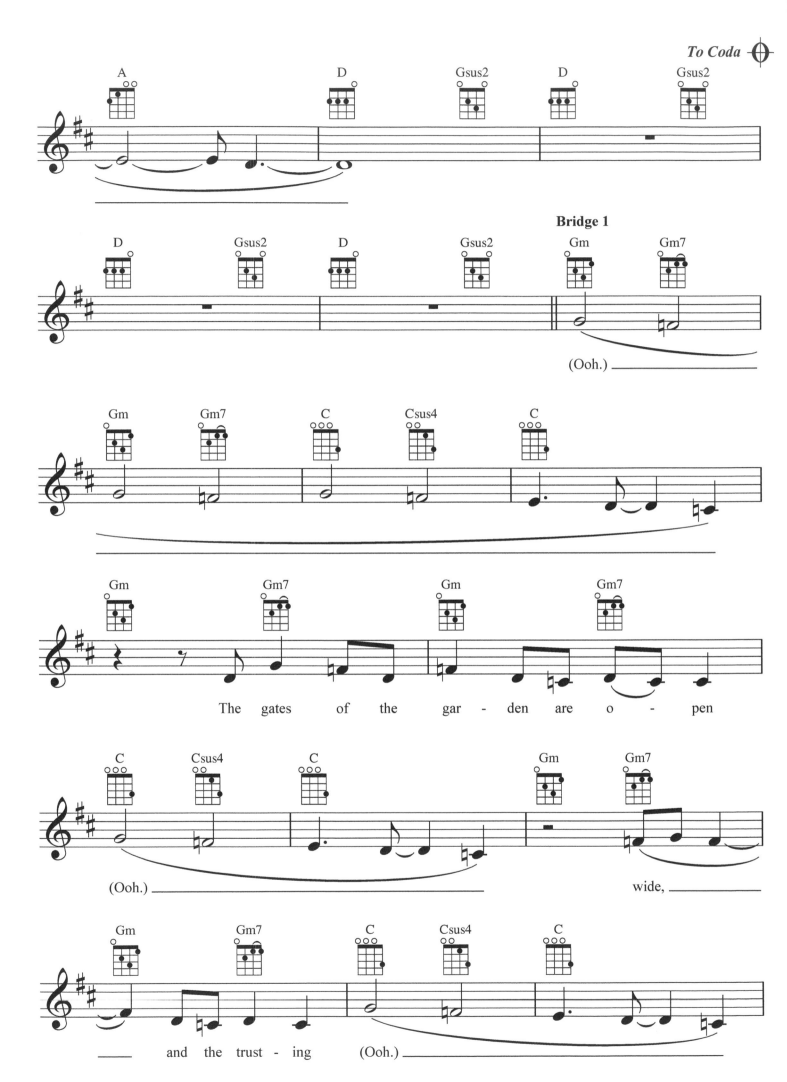

Bridge 1

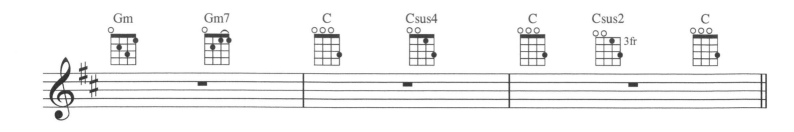

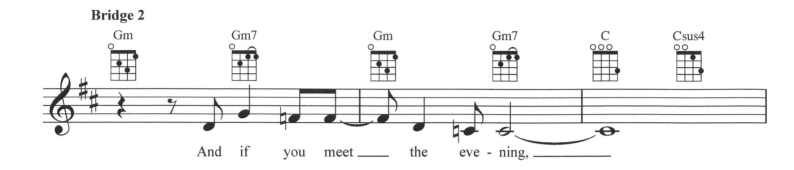

Bridge 2

And if you meet ____ the eve - ning, _____

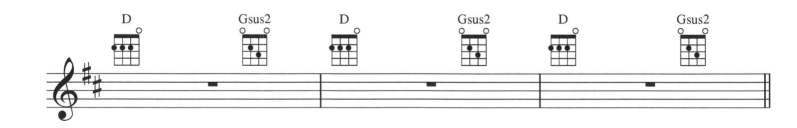

don't wait _____ for the sun ___ to rise. __

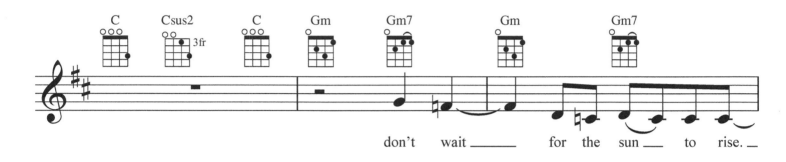

____

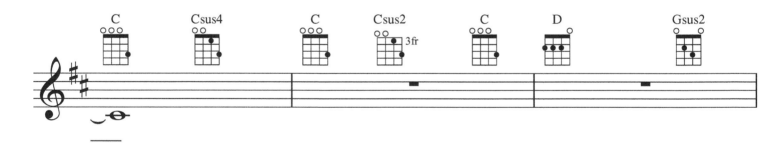

Verse

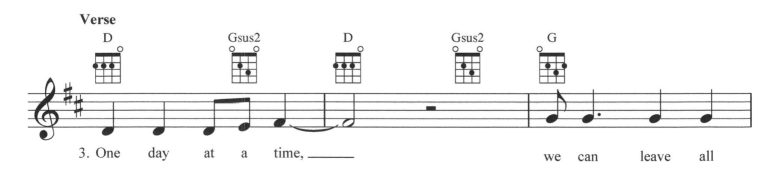

3. One day at a time, _____ we can leave all

treas - ures _____ be - hind. _____

One day at a time, _____ we can watch the clocks __

_____ un - wind. _____

Bridge 3

One day at a time, _____ a child is born __

_____ in - to _____ this world, _____ eyes blind.

One _____ day he will find his

sight   and glimpse an - oth - er kind __ of light __

____ to live   by,   one ____

day. _____

Verse

4. One   day   at   a   time, __

____ we   can   put   ma - chines ____ be - hind. ____

One   day   at   a   time, __

we can learn how birds ___

sur - vive. ___

One day at a time, ___ we can learn to fly. ___

Outro

Morning Has Broken

Words by Eleanor Farjeon
Music by Cat Stevens

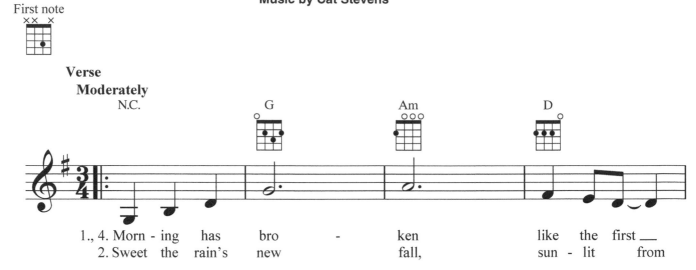

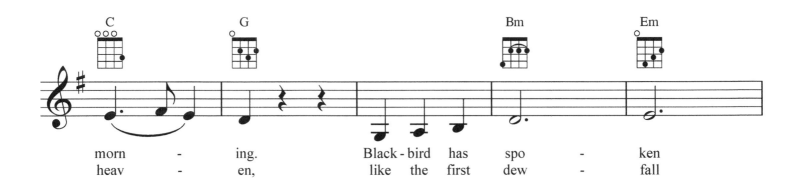

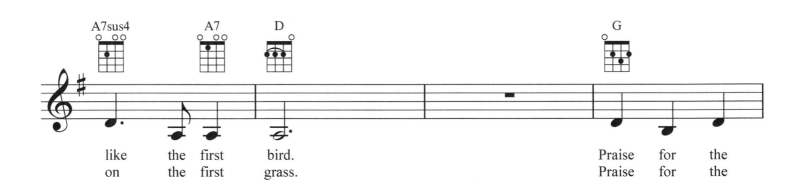

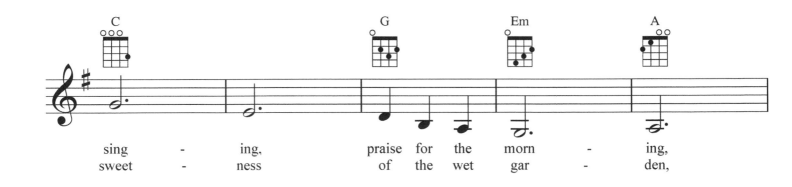

praise   for   them   spring -   ing   fresh   from   the
sprung   in   com -   plete -   ness   where   His   feet

Interlude

Word.
pass.

Verse

3. Mine is the sun - light, mine is the morn-

-ing. Born of the one

light E - den saw play. Praise with e -

la - tion, praise ev - 'ry morn - ing,

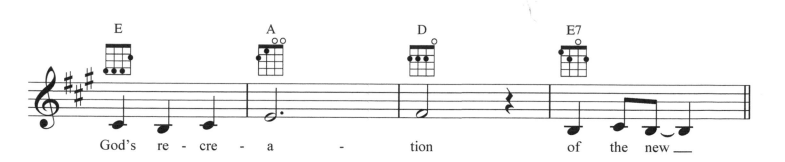

God's re - cre - a - tion of the new ___

Interlude

day.

D.C. al Fine
(take 2nd ending)

rit.

Oh Very Young

Words and Music by Cat Stevens

And though you want him to last for - ev - er, you know
en? And though you want to last _ for - ev - er, you know

he nev - er will, ___ you know he nev - er will,
you nev - er will, ___ you know you nev - er will,

and the patch - es make the good - bye hard - er still.
and the good - bye makes the jour - ney hard - er still.

1.

2. Oh, ver - y young, __

2.

Interlude

Peace Train

Words and Music by Cat Stevens

Additional Lyrics

5. Get your bags together.
   Go bring your good friends, too.
   Because it's gettin' nearer.
   It soon will be with you.

6. Oh, come and join the living;
   It's not so far from you,
   And it's gettin' nearer.
   Soon it will all be true.

7. Now, I've been cryin' lately,
   Thinkin' about the world as it is.
   Why must we go on hating?
   Why can't we live in bliss?

8. 'Cause out on the edge of darkness,
   There rides a peace train.
   Oh, peace train, take this country.
   Come take me home again.

Thinking 'Bout You

Words and Music by Yusuf Islam

First note

§ Verse

Moderately, in 2

G   C   F   C

1. When I hold your hand, ___ I could fly a
(2.) eyes, ___ I can see
3. Instrumental

F   G   C   G

zil - lion miles with you. ___ When I see your grace, ___
rain - bows in the sky. ___ Be - ing with you; ___

Em   A   B♭   G   C

I can see ___ all God's words come true. ___ Ev - 'ry lit - tle
all who ___ part - ed re - u - nite. ___ Ev - 'ry lit - tle
Instrumental ends   Ev - 'ry burn - ing

F   E7   Am   Bm7♭5   E7

bird a - bove the haze ___ and fish be - neath ___ the waves ___
pearl - drop in the clouds ___ and stones be - neath ___ the ground ___
com - et that zooms ___ and an - gels, too, ___

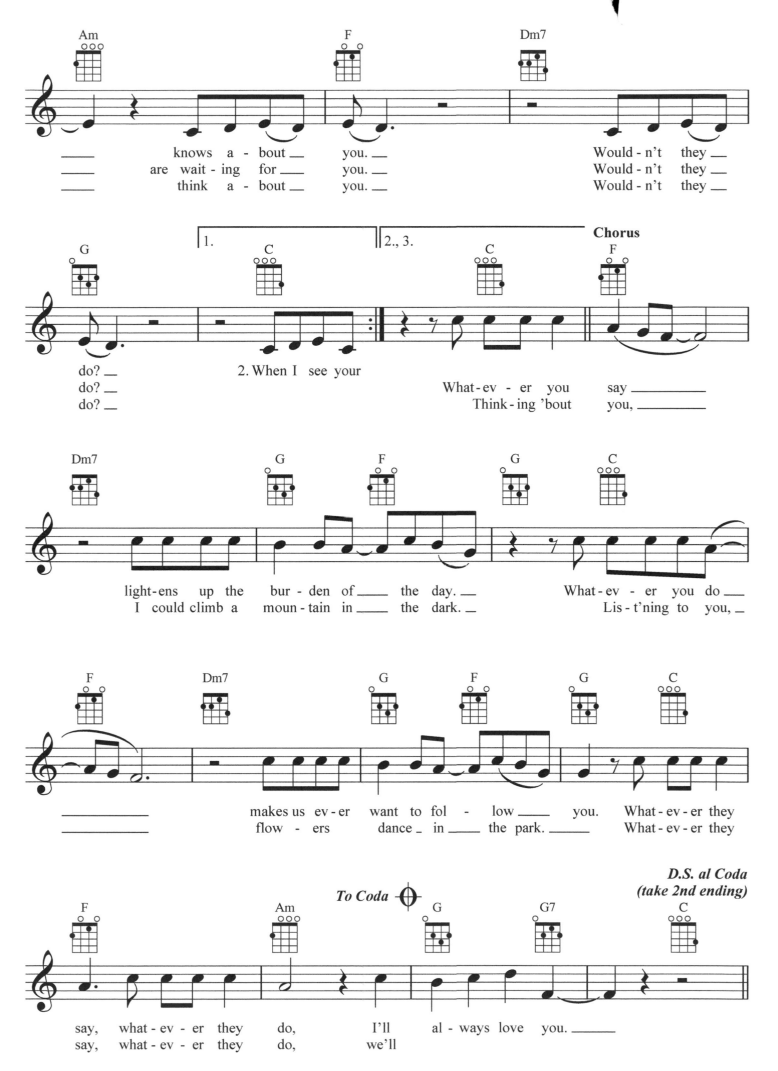

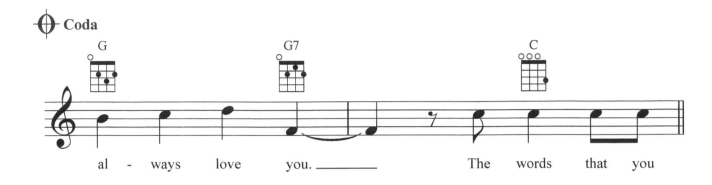

Coda

al - ways love you. _____ The words that you

Outro-Chorus

say _____

light - ens up the bur - dens of ___ the day. ___

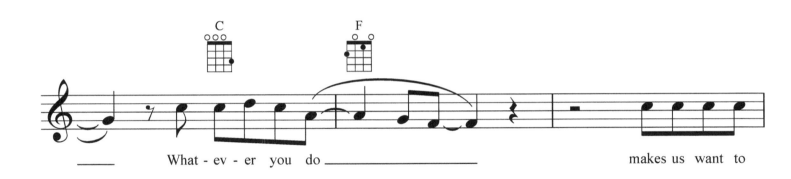

_____ What - ev - er you do _____ makes us want to

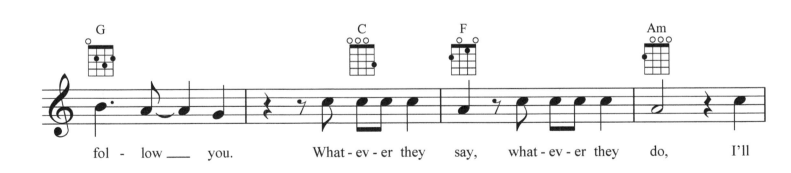

fol - low ___ you. What - ev - er they say, what - ev - er they do, I'll

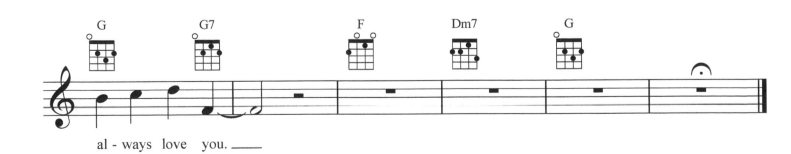

al - ways love you. ___

Roadsinger

Words and Music by Yusuf Islam

First note

Verse
Moderately fast

1. Road - sing - er came to town, ___ long cape and hat. ___
2. He stopped by a store; ___ be - tween the bar-rels and sacks, ___
3. Road - sing - er rode on to an-oth - er land. ___

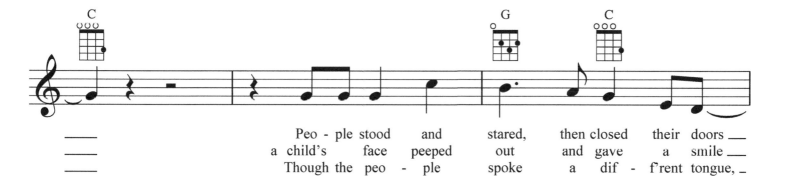

___ Peo - ple stood and stared, then closed their doors ___
___ a child's face peeped out and gave a smile ___
___ Though the peo - ple spoke a dif - f'rent tongue, ___

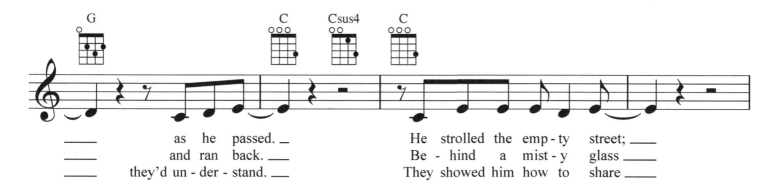

___ as he passed. ___ He strolled the emp - ty street; ___
___ and ran back. ___ Be - hind a mist - y glass ___
they'd un - der - stand. ___ They showed him how to share ___

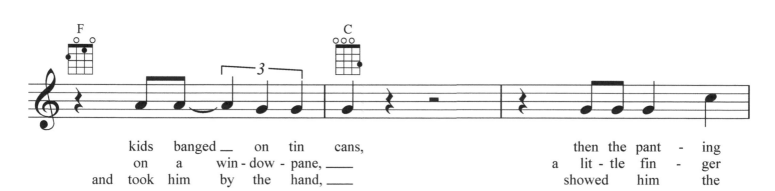

kids banged ___ on tin cans, then the pant - ing
on a win - dow - pane, ___ a lit - tle fin - ger
and took him by the hand, ___ showed him the

and the light of truth __ is blown out ____ and the roads are blocked? __
and the light of truth __ is blown out ____ and the night is cold? ____
and ev-'ry-bod - y's lost _____ look-ing for theirs? ___

(Hum)

Interlude

To Coda

D.C. al Coda   **Coda**

Where Do the Children Play

Words and Music by Cat Stevens

But tell me: __ where do the chil - dren play? _____

2. Well, you

Verse

roll on roads __ o - ver fresh, green grass for your

lor - ry loads pump - ing pet - rol gas. And you

make them long __ and you make them tough, __ but they

just go on ___ and on, and it seems that you can't get off. __

Chorus

I know we've come a long way; — we're chang-ing day — to day. —

But tell me: — where do the chil-dren play? _____

Verse

3. Well, you've cracked the sky; — scrap-ers

fill the air. — But will you keep on build-ing high-er till there's no more room

up there? Will you make us laugh? Will you

Wild World

Words and Music by Cat Stevens

First note

Verse
Moderately slow

1. Now that I've lost _____ ev - 'ry - thing to _____
2. You know, I've seen a lot of what the world can _____
3. *Instrumental*

you, _____ you say you wan - na start some - thing _____
do, _____ and it's break - ing my heart in _____

new, _ and it's break - ing my heart; _ you're leav - ing. Ba - by, I'm griev - ing.
two, _ be - cause I nev - er wan - na see you sad, girl. Don't be a bad _ girl.
Instrumental ends Ba - by, I love _ you.

(1.) But if you wan-na leave, take good care. Hope you have a lot of nice things to wear, _
(2., 3.) But if you wan-na leave, take good care. Hope you make a lot of nice friends out there, _

but then, a lot of nice things turn bad out there. ⟩
but just re - mem - ber there's a lot of bad and be - ware. ⟩

𝄋 Chorus

Ooh, ba - by, ba - by, it's a wild world.

It's hard to get by _____ just up - on a smile.

Ooh, ba - by, ba - by, it's a wild world.

I'll al - ways re - mem - ber you like a child, girl. _____

child, girl. _____

child, girl. _____

The Wind

Words and Music by Cat Stevens

1. I lis - ten to the wind, to the wind of my
2. I lis - ten to my words, but they fall far be -

soul.
low.

Where I'll end up, well, I think ___ on - ly God ___ real - ly knows. ___
I ___ let ___ my mu - sic take me where my heart ___ wants to

___ go.

I've sat up - on the set - ting sun,
I've swam up - on the dev - il's lake,

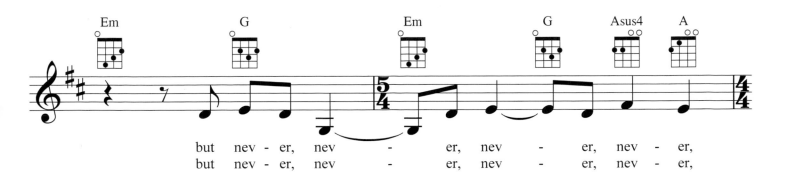

but nev - er, nev - - er, nev - - er, nev - er,
but nev - er, nev - - er, nev - - er, nev - er,

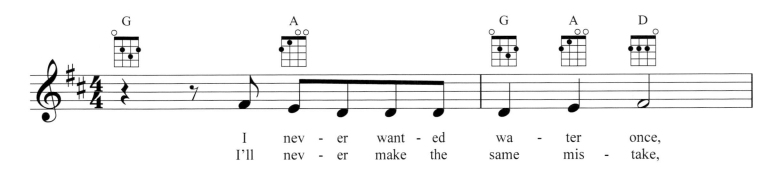

I nev - er want - ed wa - ter once,
I'll nev - er make the same mis - take,

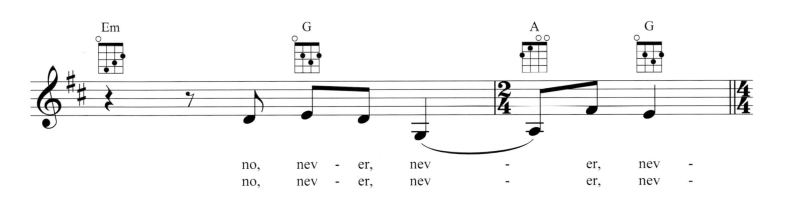

no, nev - er, nev - - er, nev -
no, nev - er, nev - - er, nev -

Interlude

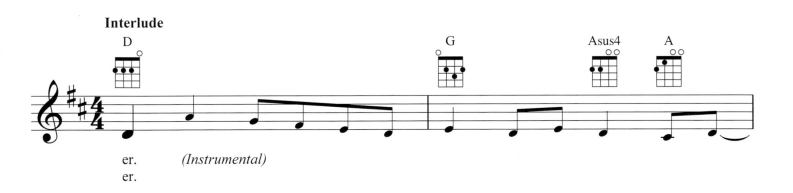

er. *(Instrumental)*
er.

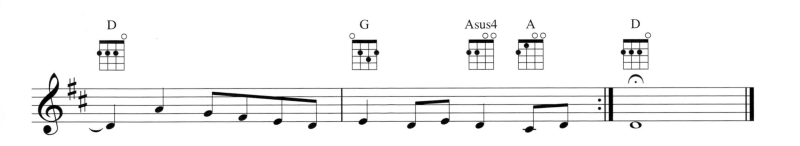

Tuesday's Dead

Words and Music by Cat Stevens

1. If I make __ a mark in time, I can't say __ the mark
2., 3. *See additional lyrics*

is mine. I'm on - ly __ the un - der - line

of the __ word. __ Yes, I'm like him, just __

__ like you. __ I can't tell __ you what to do. Like

ev - 'ry - bod - y else, I'm search - ing through what I've __ heard. __

Chorus

Whoa, ___ whoa, where do you go when you don't ___ want no one to know? Who ___ told ___ ___ to-mor-row Tues-day's ___ dead? ___

Verse

ev-'ry sec-ond on the nose, the hum-drum of the

4. Now,

Additional Lyrics

2. Preacher, won't you paint my dream?
   Won't you show me where you've been?
   Show me what I haven't seen to ease my mind.
   'Cause I will learn to understand
   If I have a helping hand.
   I wouldn't make another demand all my life.

3. What's my sex, what's my name?
   All in all, it's all the same.
   Everybody plays a different game; that is all.
   Now, man may live, man may die
   Searching for the question why.
   But if he tries to rule the sky, he must fall.